# From th

## *of a*

# Mid-Century Childhood

## *Musings of Mischief and Mayhem*

# Bonnie Papenfuss

ISBN: 979-8-6828-9785-8

# Table of Contents

*"For in every adult dwells the child that was,
and in every child, the adult that will be."*

— John Connolly, *The Book of Lost Things*

# Dedication

*This book is dedicated to the memory of my late father,*
*Lloyd Allen Wyatt.*

*He kept my conscience focused on right from wrong*
*and my hands from the dangers of idleness.*
*By the example of a strong work ethic*
*he taught respect, loyalty*
*and pride in an honest day's work, thereby*
*guiding me on a path toward success and fulfillment*
*for which I will be forever grateful.*

*Thanks, Dad*

# Acknowledgements

I want to thank my friends and family for their unfailing support.

Of utmost importance, my patient husband who, once again, spent an inordinate amount of time alone while I stared at the computer screen attempting to compose stories others might find relatable and amusing.

Also, much gratitude to my beta readers, Duke Southard and Julie A. Winrich. Their expertise as writers provided me the constructive criticism and forthright feedback necessary to put the finishing touches on my manuscript.

A special shout-out of appreciation to Debbie O'Byrne (jetlaunch.net) for designing my cover and assisting with the myriad details leading to an actual book in hand.

# Introduction

Following the heartwarming success of my first book, *From the Window of God's Waiting Room*, promoting and marketing my work became an enjoyable pastime.

Then the COVID-19 pandemic erupted. All events and speaking engagements were cancelled. Safety meant staying in. But I had all this extra time on my hands. So what does a writer do with extra time? Well, they write.

My first endeavor was a poem about the virus. I've included it after this introduction since the virus itself became an important impetus for the book's creation. Then, before I delved into any further writing, I thought it beneficial to clean up my hard drive a bit.

That led to a discovery. In with old meeting minutes and yearly, digital Christmas letters I found a file I'd created decades previous and had all but forgotten about (happens with age, you know) — a running narrative of my childhood. Something I intended to leave for the three most important women in my life, my beautiful daughters.

As I began to add information to it, a question formed in my mind: Could I make this into something others of my generation might find relatable and humorous?

And so this book was born.

# COVID-19

I talk more on the phone
or convene on the Zoom

sit for hours at the keyboard
in the stillness of my room.

I've dusted and cleaned
floors worn by the broom

my pantry's well-stocked
so too much I'll consume.

But when I feel challenged
by dire feelings of doom

I get out, take a walk
enjoy the desert bloom.

The scent of orange blossoms
such sweet, sweet perfume

eases my angst
and lifts my gloom.

Yes, I just need to be patient
as awaiting life from the womb

for this crisis will pass
and my life will resume.

Bonnie Papenfuss

# In The Beginning

The year was 1949.

It was a time of postwar prosperity. Cars got bigger. So did televisions.

China became a communist country, and Russia developed the nuclear bomb.

There were, however, no significant world events on the day of my birth. Sad but true. I googled it. Neither were there any famous individuals born on August 4, 1949, though I share the day of the month with a few well-knowns such as Louis Armstrong, Billy Bob Thornton and Barack Obama.

I have no clue as to the weather conditions nor knowledge of how many hours my mother labored in the little hospital on the banks of the Rum River in Anoka, Minnesota. Even the name of the nurse who gathered my mop of dark hair into a curlicue atop my head and insisted I looked like a little Cupie doll is unknown to me. I have only my mother's retelling and a photo as testament to my "Cupie-ness."

Since I retain only vague perceptions of events before school age, I begin these stories with my first distinct memory at the age of seven. Though all incidents are true, I admit to the abundant use of tongue-in-cheek and lavish embellishment of dialogue since in absence of both the book would be quite the snooze.

So with the hope you find my words heart-warming, humorous and relatable, I open a window into my mid-century childhood.

# Not a Gift I Asked For

"Bonnie, I told you ten minutes ago to find your brother, get your coats on and be ready to go. You haven't moved. No presents will be opened until we get back, you know."

"Aw, Dad! Come on, just one?"

"No. Not until your mother and the baby are home. And your sister is the biggest gift for all of us this year, so don't count on too much under the tree, anyway."

Moments later we were in the car and on our way to the hospital. It wasn't how I wanted the morning to go. I'd not even met this little person yet, and she'd already spoiled a perfectly good holiday. There appeared little hope for the rest of my school vacation.

Mom and Dad had seemed fine with one boy and one girl. I didn't understand their need for an addition to the family. My status as the youngest had been usurped by a newcomer. I could see no benefit to this arrangement.

"How long before we get there, Dad?" I asked, as my disinterested brother leaned against the side window and let out an exasperated sigh.

"We'll be there in half an hour. Please remember your mother's been gone four days. She'll want to catch up on things around the house, but she needs to take it easy. And since the baby will occupy a good deal of her time, you both need to pitch in. Okay?"

"Yes, Dad," we chimed with a shared lack of enthusiasm.

I slumped into the cushions, imagining the remainder of the day. Poor baby Jesus would be taking a back seat to the celebration of a different newborn this Christmas morning.

# Simpler Times

"I'll beat you to the hammock," my brother shouted in challenge.

"Oh no you won't," I hollered in retort as I willed my body into overdrive.

I knew my younger, shorter legs couldn't outrun his, but it didn't stop me from trying.

Upon reaching our revered place of relaxation first, he held out the canvas with a smile of brotherly affection and said, "Go ahead, Sis, you can have the first turn."

With a gleeful giggle, I flopped down and pulled the sides up over my body, sealing myself into a canvas cocoon. He gave a few hefty shoves and I flew so high it seemed I might turn upside down.

"Do it again. Do it again," I squealed with delight.

We'd been "underfoot" that morning, and Mom had admonished us with her standard command of, "Go outside and play. I'll call you when it's time for lunch." She followed that with the most crucial, "Don't forget, if you're not here when food's on the table, you'll go hungry till supper time!"

My brother and I didn't mind being outside, running free from Mother's watchful eye. We entertained ourselves with rudimentary toys and our own imaginations. We might swing on the hammock, chase bunnies in the woods or tie a string between two empty Campbell's soup cans and play "telephone" for hours. Compromise and cooperation were key, and, of course, the most important factor — be home by mealtime.

Sometimes, today, I yearn for those simpler, less complicated times. Then I reach for my cellphone.

# My Holiday Companion

'Twas the night before Easter in the attic of our house,
Dad stepped joist to joist, being quiet as a mouse.

Atop the twisted, cellophane grass of our baskets we'd find a boxed, Palmer's Peter Rabbit hollow, milk-chocolate bunny surrounded by an assortment of Whoppers Malted Milk Balls, Bonomo's Turkish Taffy, Peeps and, of course, a treasure trove of jelly beans.

But the best part of the holiday, for me, was our tall, straw-stuffed velveteen jack rabbits. They'd be standing next to our baskets on Easter morning. Throughout the year, swaddled in an old pillowcase, they waited in the attic. Then, the night before, after we were tucked into bed, Dad would venture up through the trap door and tread with caution from one support beam to another to retrieve them.

Each was a different pastel color, had long ears standing straight up and a satin ribbon as neck adornment. That oversized stuffed toy wasn't soft and cuddly, but I loved it and carried it with me everywhere — except to Easter morning service. Mother put the kibosh on that idea.

At week's end, I always shed a few tears when Dad rewrapped my pale pink companion and returned it to its resting place.

But I looked forward to next year's appearance.

# Peace Offerings

"He started it!"

"Really, Bonnie? I don't think you're telling me the whole story."

"Yes, I am. He twisted my arm behind my back and it hurt, so I kicked him."

"He said you knocked over what he'd spent the last hour building with his new Lincoln Logs."

"Maybe I did, but only because he wouldn't come outside and play with me."

"Well, fighting never solves anything. I wish the two of you would figure that out. For now, your brother will apologize for his part in it. As for your punishment, you will be doing his chores in addition to your own this week."

"That's not fair."

"Life isn't fair, my dear. Maybe you'll give more thought to your actions next time."

"You're so mean. I hate you! I'm going to run away from home and you'll never see me again. Then you'll be sorry."

"Well, be sure to take some water with you. It's warm out there this morning."

I slammed the back door with a huff. Tears of hurt and humiliation ran down my cheeks as I sprinted toward our makeshift fort in the woods. Soon I grew thirsty and my tummy growled. I desperately wanted Mom to find me, beg me to come home and release me from further restitution. It did not happen.

As the sun rose high in the sky, guilt and sadness weighed on my conscience. I needed to make amends.

Shuffling up the path leading back to our yard, I stopped to gather a small handful of wild bluebells. Together with a few dandelions, they made a colorful bouquet with which to pad my apology.

I opened the back door to find Mother standing in the kitchen.

"You missed lunchtime."

I held out my hand. She took the flowers from me with a smile.

"I'm sorry, Mom. I love you. I didn't mean what I said."

"I know, sweetie. It's okay. I love you too. I'll put these in some water, but I think you have a chore to do, right now, don't you? Fresh garbage bags are under the sink."

"Okay, I'll do it right away."

"There'll be a sandwich waiting on the table for you."

# Out on a Limb

"This is what I want you to do, Bonnie. Hold onto the branch closest to you and step, one foot at a time, onto my outstretched hands," my uncle said with a hint of amusement.

I looked down at him. Tears of fright dampened my cheeks.

"When I've got ahold of both your feet," he continued, "I'll tell you to stiffen your legs and let go of the branch. As I lower you, just slide your hands against the trunk of the tree for balance. When you're down far enough to feel comfortable, I'll let go and you can drop to the ground. Can you do that for me?"

"I think so, but I'm scared."

"Don't be afraid. You're a strong girl. You can do this. I won't let you fall. I promise."

I adored my mother's half-brother. Every couple of years he would visit from his home in California. He was a quirky, fun-loving character and Mom brighten in his presence.

On this visit he suggested taking us kids to the Clay Hole (a local freshwater pond) for a swim at midnight when nobody else would be there. Mom didn't like the idea of such a late hour; but with a little brotherly convincing, she compromised and agreed to leave after sunset.

At the time, I was about seven or eight years old, and the thought of such an after-dark adventure excited me. While waiting for the hours to pass, I thought it best to go outside and keep from getting underfoot. I didn't want to make any mischief that might cause Mom to squelch the whole idea.

When the hour neared, Mother hollered out the back door, "Come on, Bonnie, the sun will be going down soon. You need to get your suit on and be ready to go."

I heard her, faintly, but I didn't come running. She told me later that after a thorough search of the house, she looked out the front window to see me stuck in the branches of my favorite climbing tree — an expression of terror on my face — afraid to go up or down.

So, as my uncle gave directions from below, I did exactly as he told me, one foot at a time; and, much to my delight, it worked. When I hit the ground, he stood there chuckling as I gave him a quick squeeze and ran inside to change.

At that moment, I couldn't have loved him more! And, of course, our clandestine outing to the swimming hole sealed my undying affection. I could only dream of what his next visit might bring.

# Puppy Love

"You'll need to spend some time this weekend cleaning and organizing your room, Bonnie."

"Aw, Mom, my room is fine. I straightened everything a week or so ago."

"I know, but this time you need to concentrate on freeing up some hanger space in your closet and making room for another small chest of drawers."

"My closet is fine the way it is. And why would I want another dresser I don't need?"

"Well, *you* may not need it, but your cousin will."

"My cousin? Why would my cousin need storage space in *my* bedroom?"

"Because she's going to be living with us for a short time; and, like it or not, you'll be sharing a room with her."

Well, I didn't like it. I knew it was only a matter of time before my little sister moved in, and the idea of relinquishing my privacy before then did not appeal to me.

"That's not fair," I said with defiance.

"Remember what I always say about fairness, dear?"

"Yes, Mom, life isn't fair."

"Uh-huh. So get over it. Your cousin just graduated high school and has a job downtown. By staying here, she can take the bus, avoid the expense of a car and save for her wedding the end of July.

"And, besides, you'll be happy to know she's planning to help with the baby in the evenings and on weekends. So I suggest you make the room as comfortable as you can for the limited time she'll be with us."

I hadn't seen my cousin in a couple of years, so when she arrived the following Saturday I was surprised to be greeted by a grown woman, petite and pretty, with a perfect oval face framed by gleaming, shoulder-length, wavy dark hair.

Even more striking was her handsome fiancé who towered above her. He had a smile straight out of a Colgate commercial and a voice that reminded me of Matt Dillon on my dad's favorite TV Western.

After introductions, he spent an hour or so helping his future wife get settled in our room. I watched, with curiosity, from a distance.

Before leaving, he turned to me and said, "I know she'll be in good hands here with you, Bonnie. Thank you so much for sharing your space. I'll come by for a visit every Saturday I'm able."

"You're welcome," I replied shyly, feeling my cheeks warm. "See you next weekend."

*It was going to be a good summer!*

# Insightful Opportunities

"I'm going to be out hanging clothes on the line, Bonnie. Your dad and brother are both busy with yard work, so would you watch your sister for me, please?"

"Sure, Mom. Do I need to feed her or anything?"

"No, she just finished eating and has a clean diaper. I put her down in the playpen and she's already fallen asleep."

"Okay. I'll keep an eye on her."

Alone with a toddler who couldn't rat on me. A rare opportunity. I headed for my mother and dad's bedroom.

Around our house we kids didn't wander into our parents' room on a whim. An expectation of privacy prevailed, creating an aura of mystery and intrigue.

As I stood at the foot of their bed, my eyes took in particular things of interest. The exquisite crocheted bedspread we were not allowed to sit on; Mom's baby doll with its fancy "sleep" eyes I'd been warned not to touch, sitting atop the pillows; and her plush, stuffed dachshund guarding the middle of the bedspread where the pattern made a circular design. I moved nothing for fear of exposure.

My primary target of this mission of mischief was my mother's nightstand. More specifically, what always lie there in plain sight, its pages creased to the appropriate day of the month — her Upper Room devotional pamphlet, a veritable cornucopia of insight.

By sneaking a peek at the morning missive and accompanying Bible passage, I could better prepare for the day. If the title read *Keep My Commandments* I was smart enough to mind my Ps and Qs; whereas if it said *Forgive as the Lord Hath Forgiven You* I figured I stood a good chance of redemption for any small infractions.

To my dismay, the scripture reading for the day was Deuteronomy 6:18: *And You Shall do What is Right and Good in the Sight of the Lord.*

I ran from the room to check on my sister.

# The Benefit of Burs

Unlike our lush, well-cared-for front yard, the side area more resembled a blanket of broadleaf crabgrass and dandelions interspersed with a significant smattering of sandburs. It was, however, our main place to play since the hammock, gas tank and sandbox were located there.

Running barefoot in the summer was a temptation, though I learned it unwise to do so. Getting one of those pesky pokers in my foot had been determined an unpleasant experience, so some type of covering was essential. Alas, however, even with shoes on, I regularly picked them from my laces before entering the house.

But a yard full of crabgrass and sandburs had an up side. It proved the perfect place for grasshoppers, and we had a surplus of them. My favorite pastime became catching and imprisoning the little green hoppers in one of my metal, perforated Goody hair curlers, the kind with a red plastic roller ball which snapped over the end. I'd catch those critters, stuff them in and seal their fate.

I suppose one could make a case for creature cruelty, but it was just part of our play. And, at day's end, I'd *usually* let them out.

# Get My Goat

"Cut it out, you two," Dad barked.

"But we don't have a scissor," we taunted in return.

"Stop your sass or I'll turn this car around right now."

We knew he wouldn't, but we took a short pause in the action anyway, just as a precaution.

As usual, my brother and I were squabbling in the back of the old Ford as our sister squirmed in her car seat hooked between Mother and Dad. We were on the obligatory quarterly sojourn to see my father's parents in Riceville, Iowa. It was a three-hour drive and a boring one besides. We always found stuff to fight about.

My grandparents were each a bit of a curiosity. Grandma's sewing corner, occupying a substantial portion of the small living room, intrigued me with its stacks of yarn, piles of quilt squares, and innumerable spools of thread. Grandpa was a fascination since he had only one ear, having lost the other to the iron wheel of a thrashing machine. Both were unassuming and non-demonstrative.

Though we kids spent little time inside their tiny cottage on the banks of the "Wapsi" River, we always found things to do outside. There was a big wooden wheelbarrow in which to push our baby sister, a garden we raided for ripe strawberries, and an old "dead" car to explore parked at the edge of the property. It was rusted and filthy inside, minus its doors and covered with vines. But the cats lived there. We'd crawl inside, with no concern for cleanliness, to play with the most recent litter of kittens.

There was, however, one drawback to our visits. The goats. Now don't get me wrong, I loved the furry little creatures. They craved human interaction and we enjoyed petting and cuddling them. But I had zero appreciation for their occasional contribution to Grandma's lunch table.

"How much longer before we get there, Mom," I whined.

"Just a few more miles, dear."

"Good. I need a cold drink. I hope Grandma has some of her famous lemonade ready."

"Well, if not, I'm sure she's already milked the goats this morning. There'll likely be enough fresh and chilled in the refrigerator for all of us."

"Ew, that stuff is gross, Mom."

"Now, Bonnie, it's not so terrible. If it's all your grandmother has to offer, be polite and drink it."

"Yes, Mom, I'll be polite." *I'll politely say I'm not thirsty!*

# An Unusual Stance

In our house there were two main sources of warmth. First, the large space heater in the living room. It took up sufficient floor area to have accommodated a large bookcase, was tall enough for my dad to lean his butt up against, which he did often, and kept that portion of the house toasty.

Our second source, and my favorite place to get warm was just outside my bedroom door — a large, rectangular steel grate we referred to as the floor furnace, where heat from the unit in the crawl space flowed up into that end of the house.

I was fortunate to have the room closest to the grate.

On any given winter's evening, there I'd be, legs spread, flannel nightgown billowing out around my feet as the heat made the skin of my legs feel as though I'd spent too long in the summer sun.

When I could absorb no more, and with bedcovers turned down for quick entry, I'd grab my gown tight around my legs, step back into my bedroom and snuggle posthaste under the covers, capturing enough warmth to sleep soundly through another cold winter's night.

# Our Iron Horse

"Come on. Let's play cowboys and robbers," my brother shouted. We ran through the side yard, grabbed the handles and attempted to mount the monstrosity.

It sat on four short, metal legs atop a cement platform and held hundreds of gallons of propane. A lidded area shielding the gauges and allowing the Skelgas man access protruded from the center of the giant gas can.

It wasn't the most attractive thing in our yard, though a necessity since we lived with no city utilities. But it was a fantastic place to fuel our imaginations.

My brother and I liked to pretend the tank was a horse. However, getting onto and straddling the massive reservoir was difficult. It was tall with considerable girth for our young legs. Success often required several running starts.

Once in position, we'd "ride" while holding onto the rounded handles on each end as if they were reins and pretend to chase down notorious outlaws. When we came upon the thieves, my brother would draw his Lone Ranger cap pistol from its silver-studded holster, fire a warning shot and capture the bad guys without bloodshed.

Yes, the old "horse" was the site of many a memorable make-believe adventure.

# Big Brother is Watching

"You better eat all that! I can report you to your teacher, you know. And then I'll tell Mom and Dad you're wasting their money."

He was in sixth grade and I in fourth. Because of excellent grades and *perceived* good behavior (think Eddie Haskell on Leave it to Beaver), my dear brother had been appointed lunchroom monitor. He reveled in the privilege, asserting power over the person most easily intimidated: me.

That morning I forgot to pack a cold lunch. Going through the lunch line, I was handed a bowl of chili con carne. As I gazed at the tray, I knew my midday meal was not going to be a palate-pleasing experience. School chili contained chunks of slimy cooked tomatoes. I couldn't stand to hold them in my mouth, let alone chew and swallow.

Putting the vessel aside, I concentrated on crackers and fruit. Then my brother came up behind me with his threat. Being a model student, I didn't want to get into any trouble at school. At home we were encouraged to eat everything on our plate, due to household income, an aversion to wastefulness and, of course, those "starving children in China," so I knew my parents would not be pleased.

As he continued to harass, I ate what little of the concoction I was able while holding back my emotions (and more) so as not to provide him undue gratification. My meager attempts did not satisfy.

With autocratic authority he stated, "You're going to be in so much trouble."

Returning to the classroom, I assumed he tattled on me. My tears burst forth. The teacher, seeing my distress, knelt down and inquired, "What's wrong, dear?"

I blurted out everything through my sobs. She handed me a tissue and told me in the kindest voice, "Don't you worry, honey. I'll have a talk with your brother's teacher. This won't happen again, I promise."

At home, I never mentioned the unpleasant incident — nor did my sibling.

# Tinsel Tirade

"All right, you two hooligans, stop your roughhousing."

"Aw, geez, Mom. We're just having fun," my brother said. "Besides, we've been at this for hours."

"Well, I placed my vintage angel atop the tree, so it's time for you both to add the finishing touches. Here's the bag. The task is all yours. Please give it your best effort."

"Oh, boy, I love doing the tinsel," I said as I took the container from her.

Even though the previous year we'd taken great care to store it properly, those long pieces of fragile, crinkly lead filament were in a knotted-up glob. But it didn't bother me in the slightest. I separated the strands with delicacy and draped them one by one, being careful to match the length of both ends.

My brother, however, announcing he'd already "wasted" significant play time, had no patience for such painstaking efforts. Instead, he grabbed a fistful of twisted tin, cranked back and tossed toward the tree. The bundle landed in a haphazard heap.

Noting the horror on my face he smiled slyly. "Go ahead, Sis," he said. "I know you want to, and you won't hurt my feelings one little bit."

I proceeded to pluck the wad from its precarious perch and finish the job in proper fashion.

# Is It Time Yet?

"Well, I guess I better go scrape off my whiskers," he uttered aloud.

It was Dad's standard mantra, announced over and over again at regular intervals throughout the evening, every evening from fall to spring, while standing in his particular place of preference.

My diminutive father, who tipped the scale at his highest weight of a hundred and twenty-five pounds while in the military, was often cold. Soon after supper dishes were cleared, he assumed the position. Feet, clad in heavy welder's shoes, braced slightly forward and butt firmly affixed against the toastiest thing in our house — the living room space heater.

It wasn't as if he had no comfy chair. His favorite, a swivel rocker with wooden arms and vinyl upholstery, waited nearby. Sometimes on a Saturday night when the situation on Gunsmoke got tense, he'd leave his post to sit a spell. But it wasn't long before that tiny tush returned to its previous posture.

And, like clockwork, thirty minutes later, he announced yet again, "Well, I guess I better go scrape off my whiskers."

We all glanced his way in unison to catch any possible movement.

It became quite the humorous ritual. I wondered whether his procrastination was due to some unpleasant aspect of shaving or if he just needed to soak up every possible bit of warmth.

I believe it was the latter since by the time he took up his razor I was usually cozy under the covers.

# I Wish I Could Tickle Those Ivories

"Bonnie, I haven't heard you practicing today."

"Aw, Mom. I promise I'll do it right after I finish my math assignment."

"Okay, but I expect you to be done before dinner. Remember, you promised to work on your lesson a half hour each day. Improvement won't happen without practice, you know."

It was a daily litany between us. I found doing my arithmetic homework more appealing than playing the piano. Neither of my parents, to my knowledge, had any significant musical expertise on the complicated instrument. I didn't understand why they thought I had potential for it.

Regardless, every Saturday I walked to my instructor's house for a grueling hour-long session on the keyboard. As a teacher, she was quiet, patient and sweet-tempered, but my lack of interest caused her frequent frustration.

After two years of torturous tutoring and failing to advance beyond the basics, I quit.

Over the years I have regretted my immature absence of commitment. Even though I showed no glowing natural aptitude, I believe, with a more serious degree of dedication, I could have gained an acceptable level of competency on those ivory keys.

Playing the piano is a talent I've often wished I possessed.

# Favorites

"**M**om, can we stop right away to see our three cousins?"

"No, Bonnie, we're going to visit with your grandparents first. Afterward, we'll grab a bite of supper in town and get ourselves settled for the night. We can see them in the morning before heading home. Okay with you?"

"I guess."

"And, besides, I have a hunch it's as much your uncle you want to see as it is the girls. Am I right?"

"Well, yes."

"That's sweet of you, Bonnie. I know he enjoys our visits as much as you kids do."

A good portion of my father's extended family lived in and around Riceville, Iowa. It was a long drive, so we'd break up the trip with an overnight, either at the local motel or with my dad's brother and his wife who had no children and sufficient room for all of us.

While in town we often dropped in on other aunts and uncles. They were all nice and I didn't dislike any of them. But some relatives were just more kid-friendly. I'm not embarrassed to say there was one I loved above all others.

My dad's brother, the one closest to him in age, lived smack-dab in the hub of downtown, if you could call a cafe, church, motel, bar and service station a hub. He and my aunt had daughters close in age to the three of us.

29

Eighteen months separated the two brothers. Both were slight in build and short in stature with facial features so similar they had, on occasion, been mistaken for twins.

One important difference, however, set them apart. My father was quiet and "buttoned-up," while his sibling, more demonstrative and easygoing. The lines on his face were testament to an ear-to-ear smile that could light up a room and warm the heart of any child in his presence.

The next morning, when our car lumbered into the driveway, Uncle greeted us kids with a group bear hug. Upon release, I turned and felt his arms encircle my waist. He twirled me once, twice, three times around. My legs flew free as I shrieked with delight.

"How've you been, Squirt? Long time no see," he stated with a grin while I wobbled to regain my equilibrium.

As we headed for the house, Uncle playfully rubbed his knuckles atop my head.

*Oh, yes, I knew who my favorite was.*

# Holiday "Feast"

"Hey, Bonnie. You wouldn't be gobbling that down so fast if you knew what you were eating," my sibling jeered.

I ignored his brotherly badgering, enjoying the fact we were all spending Easter dinner with two of my favorite relatives.

Dad's sister and her husband were hardworking farm folks who lived in an older home with few modern conveniences. But they were good to us kids, and if one could get past the negatives of visiting them — a terrifying greeting by a gaggle of geese primed to snap at your shins and an outdoor biffy requiring a sturdy stick with which to knock down the potty protrusion to avoid it tickling one's tush — the positives were quite enjoyable.

When not dressed for a special occasion, I'd run to the pig pen in the back acreage of the property and talk a while with my farm favorite — a smallish, one-eared sow I named Pinky. Over the years, I grew quite attached to the little porker.

Often during our visits, my brother and I hooked a lead rope to the halter of Uncle's aging draft horse, gave each other a leg up and took turns riding bareback as the big old Clydesdale plodded around the pasture.

"So," my brother continued to taunt, "I'm just going to tell you. You're feasting on that ugly pig you liked so much."

I assumed he was teasing, until I looked across the table at my uncle's apologetic eyes.

Tears ran down my cheeks. *Oh, poor, precious Pinky!*

# My Canine Conundrum

"Mom. Mom. Come quick!"

"For goodness' sake, Bonnie, what's so urgent?"

"I chipped a tooth."

"Oh my, what were you doing to cause that?"

"I was hungry, so I got a carrot from the refrigerator. When I bit down, a piece of my tooth broke off."

"Really? You were eating a carrot? Are you sure you weren't opening those bobby pins with your teeth again after I've told you so many times not to?"

"No, Mom. I swear."

"Well, let me take a peek," she said as I opened for inspection. "Hmm, at least it isn't a permanent tooth. I'll call tomorrow and see if we can get you in next week."

Though I had my share of tooth issues, I never minded going to the dentist. He'd always have a smile and a joke for us kids and a tiny TV mounted above the spittle bowl tuned to a comedy show for our entertainment.

When I sat in the exam chair a few days later, the doctor said, "Now, Bonnie, let's see what we have here. Your mom says you chipped this on a carrot. Is that right?"

I glanced over at my mother sitting by the door. Her brows were raised as she peered at me over the top of her glasses.

"Uh-huh," I responded with an open mouth.

"Well, the tooth is definitely rotten enough to have broken from the pressure of biting into something hard. But it's pretty loose now and needs to come out. Today."

I did not like having teeth pulled — by me or anyone else. However, since the good doctor had unwittingly kept my secret, the pain was a price I was willing to pay.

# Second Chances

"I need a little help," he hollered.

A minute passed.

"I need a little help." This time, a hint of desperation.

By now I was wide awake.

"I need a little help." Louder. The anguish, palpable.

I heard her footsteps, in what had become an every-night ritual, pad the length of our house to the far bedroom — my bedroom, which I'd already shared for a short time with a cousin, now relinquished to my grandfather.

Growing up, my mother had never experienced a close relationship with her dad. Using a method of marital separation not uncommon in those days, he had taken up residence in an old cabin on property the family owned across the road from the main house.

Mom told us kids of the time her teacher sent a note home indicating the need for glasses. Her mother had said, "Well, dear, you know I only have enough money for household expenses. Go discuss this with your father. Maybe he'll agree to pay for your eyeglasses."

She explained how nervous she'd been while walking the long driveway. She was relieved when, after stating her case, he'd agreed to provide the necessary funds.

Grandpa spent his life in the little shack in the woods, insulated from the rest of the world. Following a major stoke, however, he could no longer live by himself. My parents, after considerable deliberation, decided he should stay with them and Mom would care for him to the best of her ability.

I believe, in this case, my mother, youngest of the eight full siblings, saw a chance to hone a more intimate connection with a father she scarcely knew. She took on the challenge with dutiful devotion.

At the time, I was too young to grasp the family dynamics involved, but old enough to sense some initial discomfort. Things seemed to become easier as months went on.

Except for the noisy midnight bathroom breaks and the fact I had to share a room with my brother, it was nice to have a grandparent in the house. Sometimes, he would summon us kids and joke around in his gruff and gravely old-man voice. I think he just wanted to get to know his grandchildren. I loved him for the effort.

As time wore on, Grandpa's worsening condition necessitated a move to the nursing home. He passed away soon after. I was ten years old, but the time we'd spent together provided me many memories I cherish.

I believe the same could be said for my mother.

# Door Dilemma

"But I don't want to sleep there, Mom! Why can't we get a room at the little motel across from the gas station. We did one other time, remember?"

"Yes, but it was a family reunion when houses were full with other relatives. We had no choice. We always stay at your uncle's house when we're visiting your dad's folks. I don't understand what's gotten into you. I thought you loved your aunt and uncle."

"I do. They're great. Uncle jokes around with us kids, and Auntie makes sure there are always fresh-baked chocolate chip cookies on the counter. I like being at their house and playing in the little shed in the back yard."

"Then what's the problem? Why don't you want to be there overnight? You and your brother enjoy sleeping on the screened-in porch. You say it's like camping out. What's made you so hesitant? Just tell me and I'll try to take care of whatever it is."

"This is not something you can fix, Mom."

"Well, you're being difficult, Bonnie. If you won't explain yourself, there's no reason to continue this discussion."

How could I tell her? She would not understand. My mother lacked any bashfulness about these things. Growing up in a family of eight children often meant time together in the two-holer with another sibling. There'd been no room for modesty.

I did not share my mother's lack of timidity. The toilet in my aunt's house made me uncomfortable. It had two doors. One exited to the living area and the other to the main bedroom. Only the first locked. I was ashamed to admit the negative effect this had on my psyche.

So real was my fear, I refused any beverage offered after the supper hour. I knew from experience, a nighttime visit to their washroom could cause my usual shy bladder to be downright recalcitrant, creating a longer stay and a greater likelihood of unintentional interruption. I made every attempt to avoid the need to void.

All this led to a decision. If ever I had occasion to own a home with two doors leading into a bathroom, each would have a lock!

# My Dream Come True

A mature oak tree with branches configured to provide the perfect roosting spot stood at the far edge of our front yard, closest to the highway.

At about ten years of age, one of my favorite pastimes was to climb up and sit for hours watching the big-finned, rocket-shaped, chromed-out cars of the 50s whiz by. There was the iconic 57 Chevy Bel Air, the 58 Packard coupe with its double fins and the 59 Chevy Impala sporting a curvy aerodynamic design.

But my ultimate favorite of the "gas-guzzling boats" — as my conservative father insisted upon calling them — was the one with the biggest, tallest and most elaborate fins of all: the 1959 Cadillac Eldorado. I dreamed of someday owning one.

Over the years, I held onto my fascination with old cars, especially those built before 1960. I'll still drag my husband to car shows and often, much to his chagrin, stop to admire a vintage vehicle parked in a grocery or drug store parking lot.

As my life unfolded, I did purchase, and still own, a 1959 Cadillac Eldorado. Several to be honest.

And they all look quite nice together on my china cabinet shelf.

# A Mother Knows

"Can I please take your new Parents magazine into my room, Mom?"

"*Can* you? I think you're *able*. But that's not the question, is it?"

"I'm sorry. *May I* take it into my room, please?"

"Have you finished your weekend homework? Do you need any help? Last week you struggled with some long-division problems."

"I remember, Mom. This time they weren't hard. And the only other thing was an English assignment. I had to compose a paragraph or two about my summer vacation. You know how much I love to write, so that was a cinch."

"Yes, dear, you like to write. I am well aware."

"So would it be okay if I borrowed the magazine for a while? I enjoy the stories and sometimes I even learn stuff about helping around the house. I know you have your hands full with a toddler running around."

"Well, I have a feeling your motives are not as selfless as you claim, but that's fine. I'm done with the latest issue. You're free to take it for a few days if you like. Just remember to return it to the living room."

"I will, I promise. Thanks, Mom."

I grabbed the magazine and headed for the privacy of my bedroom. In truth the stories didn't interest me. I wanted to look for a particular advertisement I'd seen in one of the previous issues.

Flipping through, I spotted it right away. The wording read: *Would You Like to Write Children's Books?* It went on to say those interested should submit an idea for a book in 500 words or less. All entries would be considered. The winner would get an opportunity to work with an editor and possibly have his or her story published.

This was my chance. I'd write the perfect children's story and win the contest. My words would someday be in the hands of little kids around the country, maybe even the world!

I considered a couple of different ideas. Then it hit me. The story line would revolve around an unusual friendship between a cat and a canary. It would be a feel-good lesson in cooperation and the appreciation of differences.

I wrote and rewrote all afternoon. Then I completed the final copy in my best penmanship. Emerging from seclusion, I strode to the living room, chest out and head held high.

"I put the magazine back on the coffee table, Mom," I announced.

"Oh," she said with a hint of surprise. "I did say you could keep it for a few days, didn't I?"

"Yes, but I'm done already."

"All right. Did you come upon anything of interest? Maybe an article on the best way for an older sibling to entertain a three-year-old?"

"Um, no. But I did find what I was looking for."

"Really? And what was that?"

"An ad for writers."

"Yes, and so?"

"Well, they need people to create children's books. It's a contest. So I wrote a story and I want to send it in. I know it's good. I plan to win and get published."

"Well, you've set yourself a pretty high bar, Bonnie. I know it's your dream to author a book someday, but you're very young. Do you think they'll even consider something a child sends in?"

"I didn't see an age requirement, Mom."

"Okay. But still, I don't want you to get your hopes up and then be disappointed."

"I promise I won't be crushed if I don't win. Could I *please* just have an envelope and a stamp?"

"Well, I guess there's no harm in trying. They're in the desk, honey. Just help yourself."

"Oh, Mom, thanks. You're the best!"

After stamping and addressing the envelope, I walked it to the mailbox. As I raised the little red flag, I imagined my words traveling all the way to New York City and being read by some famous editor at a prestigious publishing house.

The wait to contest deadline seemed never-ending. Then another week went by, and another and another. I'd given up hope when one afternoon, as I was sitting at the table pretending to concentrate on my arithmetic, Mother came in from outside with an envelope in her hand.

"There's a letter here for you, Bonnie. It looks official."

I scanned the return address. This was it. The long-awaited notification.

My hands trembled as I tore open the flap and unfolded the typed page within. It began: "First I want to thank you for taking the time to submit an entry for our contest . . . your writing flowed well . . . and the plot was quite intriguing . . ."

I skipped to the bottom.

"Unfortunately, you are too young to be considered for publication, but please don't be discouraged. Keep writing and continue striving toward your goals."

It was signed by someone with a couple of official titles following his name.

"What does it say?" Mom asked.

"You were right," I said, trying not to sound upset. "I'm not old enough."

"Oh, I'm so sorry, honey."

"At least the person who wrote the letter said my work 'flowed well' and the story idea was interesting. He encouraged me to keep writing."

"Well, good. He's right, you know. Continue to follow your dream. Someday your name will grace the cover of a book. I'm sure of it."

# Noisy Horns & Pointy Hats

Not at our house. No horns nor hats, that is.

Birthdays were no big deal. Mother didn't spend the week cleaning and shopping in preparation. She didn't plan children's games, stock up on party favors or string crepe-paper streamers in anticipation of a celebration.

Of course we were acknowledged on our special day. We'd get a couple of gifts — one always an item of necessity — and Mom would bake our favorite chocolate layer cake to share for after-dinner dessert, with vanilla ice cream, for sure.

But there wasn't a big hoo-ha made of the day. No gaggle of school chums to pummel a piñata or join in an overnight with playful pillow fights.

It was a simple matter of time and cost for both host and attendee. My parents felt it impractical and inconsiderate to expect others to sacrifice precious time carting their child to and from a birthday function. In addition, they objected to anyone having to incur the cost of a gift for a progeny not their own.

Parties were not prudent. That was the way of it, and likely a good lesson in both frugality and humility.

To this day, due to both personality and pocketbook, I much prefer to forego frivolity for more sedate and intimate gatherings with family and friends.

# Queen For a Day

"Hey, Bonnie, I need to talk to you," he shouted as he banged on the door.

I was enjoying a morning tea party with the neighbor girl. Her playhouse was a thing of beauty with little wooden chairs, windows that opened and miniature china dishes. Mine consisted of a small clearing in the woods, two old peach crates and numerous kitchen discards.

Already I'd heard the details of her trip to the State Fair the day before and how she'd gone on "every single ride." Our family had only ever attended the lame county fair.

Then, to top things off and since it occupied a prominent place at our tea-party table, I'd learned all about her new, life-size Patti Playpal doll. I was envious, but tried to hide it.

She was not my favorite playmate, since she seemed to derive pleasure from making me feel inferior. But given her close proximity, I would often put aside my pride and suffer the humiliation to have someone to play with other than my baby sister.

"Come on, Bonnie," my brother continued to demand. "You have to come home. Right now!"

"Why? I just got here. We're having fun. What's the big emergency?"

"I can't tell you. It's a surprise."

"Right," I said, with a tone of distrust.

"You don't believe me?"

"What do you think?"

"Okay, fine, I'll tell you. Mom and Dad are taking us to the State Fair today."

"Really? You're not just saying that?"

"I'm telling you the truth. We're all going. Now come on. And, remember, you better act surprised!"

At that moment, I could not have felt more privileged if someone had placed a diamond-studded tiara on my head and crowned me Queen of England.

I puffed out my chest, turned to my neighbor and with a somewhat haughty air stated, "I'm sorry, I have to go now. If I'm not too tired from all the excitement of the fair, maybe I'll come over tomorrow."

Thirty minutes later, we were bound for the Great Minnesota Get-Together. I knew the rest of the day would be dazzling.

But the morning had already been spectacular!

# Belle of the Neighborhood

"Rides for a nickel," my brother shouted as we wove Lulu up and down the streets of a nearby housing area.

My parents' original plan had been to get us each a horse, since, in their estimation, the work involved with owning one would keep our hands busy and out of trouble.

But Dad thought it might be smart to start us on something a bit smaller. With a burro we could learn to ride, but not have as far to fall. It would teach us responsibility and provide good company for horses when or if he decided we were ready for them. So Lulubelle took up residence in our little barn.

Though patient as we learned to ride, it became evident Lulu enjoyed pulling as much as she did having someone on her back. It wasn't long before Dad had our mild-mannered jenny harnessed to a small, hand-made wooden cart with seats on each side.

In preteen entrepreneurial fashion, my brother and I decided our burro and her cart could provide the perfect vehicle with which to pad our piggy banks.

Soon the rattle of harness clips and the clogging of Lulu's hoofs on asphalt brought the neighborhood kids running from their front doors faster than the jingle of the Good Humor man.

# Shared Interest

"Are all the perishables in the cooler?" Dad asked.

"Yes, and what isn't going to spoil I've stacked on the counter. It should be easier to move around now."

"Good," he said. "This old refrigerator hasn't been working as efficiently as it should for some time. With a new motor, things'll be much better."

"That sure will be nice," Mom said.

"I'll have it swapped out and cooling in a couple of hours. Stuff should be okay in the ice chest for that long."

My dad, even without the advantage of a high-school education, could design, build, fix or restore almost anything. He had an uncanny ability to visualize things in three dimensions. And as far as engine repair, whether it be lawnmower, refrigerator, airplane or car, there was no one more skilled than my father.

I was sitting at the dining room table finishing some homework during the icebox discussion. It didn't take long before the unit was pulled from the wall, its power disconnected and my dad busy removing the dying motor.

A short time later, he came to the table holding the innards of the old Frigidaire. "Are you finished with your schoolwork, Bonnie?" he asked.

"Yes, I'm getting ready to put my books away right now."

"Well, I know how much you like to tinker and learn how parts fit and move together, so if you want, I'll find you an extra screwdriver and pliers, and you can explore the workings of this old thing."

"Sure," I said. "That would be great!"

After Mom put an old towel down to safeguard her precious oak table, I began dismantling. The parts were small with numerous nuts and bolts to remove. I was deep into it when I heard Dad cuss in frustration.

"For Christ's sake," he hollered. "They sold me the wrong motor. This doesn't fit our refrigerator!"

I stopped, mid-bolt.

"Bonnie," he said, approaching the table, "I need to — "

With raised eyebrows and gaping mouth, he surveyed the array of loose parts and pieces. I held my breath, concerned for his reaction.

"Well," he sighed, "this'll be a challenge. But I need to put the old motor back together and reinstall it so we have something, at least, to keep our food from going to waste."

He didn't scold me. And he did get it up and running again. I knew he would.

# Aw, Rats!

"Well, students, the school year is coming to a close, and the nutrition study with our two rodents is over," announced my fifth-grade teacher. "It's now up to you children to find these animals good homes."

We looked around at one another with questioning eyes. *What did she mean? How were we, a bunch of kids, supposed to find them new homes?*

"Tonight I want all who are interested to ask your parents if it would be okay for you to adopt one of the white rats," she continued. "If your mom and dad are agreeable, bring a note stating their permission. Tomorrow, I'll put all the slips in a hat and pull out two names. Those students will then choose whether they want Pixie or Dixie."

One of the boys shouted, "Hot diggity dog!" Our expressions of confusion turned to joyful anticipation. It seemed everyone in the room wanted one of those red-eyed rodents for their very own, including me.

I formulated a plan on the long bus ride home. As soon as the front door closed behind me, I blurted out what the teacher told us.

"Please, please, Mom. They are so cute. I promise I'll take good care of it."

Mother hesitated, a thoughtful expression on her face.

"Slow down, Bonnie. Tell me again about your project with these creatures."

"Well," I began, "we fed Dixie junk food and Pixie healthy greens and vitamins. So now one of them is skinny and tired all the time and the other is plump and eager to play. It taught us how important it is to follow a healthy diet."

"Hmm, a good lesson, indeed," she replied. "So you're supposed to bring a permission slip tomorrow if we agree you can have one of the animals. Then the teacher will pull out two names. Correct?"

"Yes, that's right. Oh, please, Mom, please. Can I? Can I?"

"And you say many of the students in your class are planning to ask their parents?"

"Yes, of course. All the kids want one!"

"Well, I'll talk it over with your father. But I can't say I'm too excited about the idea. A small animal is as much work as a big one, Bonnie. Are you sure you want the added responsibility?"

"Oh yes, Mom, I promise I'll do all the work. I'll feed it and clean its cage every week and Sis can play with it too. They're so cute, Mom. Please."

"Your sister would like that, I'm sure. However, I'm still not convinced. As I said, your father and I will discuss it after he gets home and we've all had dinner. Whatever decision we come to will be our final word on the matter. Do you understand?"

"Yes, Mom, but please tell Dad what I said."

"I will, but I make no promises. Now get busy on your homework."

Dad arrived two hours later. Dinnertime seemed to last forever. Afterward, I cleared the table and did the dishes without being asked.

When Mother and Dad emerged from their closed-door, post-mealtime discussion, they were smiling. My heart pounded as I waited for their answer.

"Well, Bonnie, your dad and I have talked it over at great length, and we've agreed to write you a permission slip."

My entire body shook with excitement! "Oh, thank you, thank you!"

"However," she cautioned, "we don't want you to be disappointed if it's not your name the teacher announces."

"I won't be. I promise."

At the time I didn't fully comprehend the depth of discussion during their parental powwow. Only after I got off the bus the following afternoon, proudly toting a small cage containing one healthy, hairless-tailed white rat, did I begin to decode their thought process.

One look at me and my mother stood dumbstruck. After regaining her voice she asked, "So, Bonnie, your name was picked from *all* those others?"

"Not really," I said. "Our teacher didn't have to draw names."

"What are you talking about, child?"

"Well, only Danny and I brought notes. So we each got one. He was nice enough to let me choose first and I picked the lively one, Pixie."

"Oh, for heaven's sake," my mother exclaimed. "Your father and I assumed every one of those kids would bring a permission slip. He is not going to be happy about this."

*Aha! The truth. They'd gambled on so many names being in the hat, I wouldn't stand a chance. Surprise!*

# Head Above Water

"Well, hello again, Bonnie. Good to have you back. I'm glad you're going to give it another try. I have a feeling this is the year you'll find the confidence to take the big leap."

That was Miss Hazel's pep talk before I started yet another summer session of lessons at the local swimming hole. She was a kind and patient teacher, though over the years I tested her composure.

Because my mother lost a young brother to a boating accident, she was immovable in the resolve we kids learn to swim proficiently and confident in Hazel's ability to make it happen.

I didn't share her optimism. I could dog paddle the required distance back and forth and, with limited expertise, demonstrate the different strokes. But I needed to pass the final hurdle in order to receive my completion certificate.

It terrified me to have my face in the water or my head under it for any length of time. And that fear had been exacerbated by a near-drowning incident at church camp.

We were in the middle of the lake on a pontoon platform. I went down the ladder and was treading water close to the safety of the raft when, without warning, someone cannonballed, landed on my head and pinned me under for what seemed like an eternity. It was a terrifying experience.

So the prospect of diving from a bouncy board high in the air and ending up submerged for any period of time was a horrifying thought. Year after year I watched kids much younger climb the steps with courage, pad out to the point of no return and dive with dogged determination into the abyss.

Not me. It never happened.

I was destined to forever keep my head above water.

# Silence, Please!

"Children should be seen and not heard."

You're familiar with the saying, right?

Being a quiet and obedient child myself, the requirement was not a significant imposition, except at mealtime.

I'm not referring to whether we were allowed to speak at the table. If there was something of import we progeny needed to impart, it was acceptable. What we could not do was make any sort of eating noises.

My father held the notion there should be no discernible sound associated with the task of consuming one's food. You may think that's only polite; and, to a point, I would agree. It's true, when enjoying a meal the last thing one wants is to be subjected to the open-mouthed smacking of a fellow tablemate. Eating in such a manner, in my opinion, shows a lack of proper upbringing.

But Dad's grievances went much deeper. He believed there should be no sound whatsoever. Not when chewing. Not when swallowing. And if he heard something, he squinted his eyes and furrowed his brow in distain as the guilty perpetrator suffered "the look."

Aside from the obvious obstacles associated with items such as apples or corn flakes (I opted for bananas and Cream of Wheat), the most challenging part was drinking.

Have you ever attempted to imbibe a beverage, any beverage, silently? It's almost impossible to prevent your throat from making a slight, almost imperceptible glugging sound.

With sufficient practice, however, it is an attainable skill, and, out of nothing more than sheer survival, one at which I became quite proficient.

# Leaves of Three . . .

"For goodness' sake, Bonnie. Stop fidgeting at the breakfast table. What's gotten into you, anyway?"

"I'm sorry, Mom. My legs feel all scratchy, and I have some little red spots."

"Hmm, spots? Let's go in your bedroom and I'll have a look."

The day before, I'd spent the night at my grandma's house. She lived in Elk River, only a short drive away, so we visited often. I loved staying with her during summer vacation. There were freedoms allowed at her place which were frowned upon at mine, and she always planned something special for us to do together.

"My heavens!" Mother exclaimed. "Exactly what did you and Mom do yesterday?"

"Oh, we had the best time. Grandma and I walked to the far end of the pasture and had a picnic. We ate fried chicken, homemade biscuits and — "

"Stop right there. A picnic?"

"Uh-huh. It was so much fun."

"By chance, did your grandmother mention seeing any poison ivy?"

"Well, yes, I think so, but she flattened everything before we spread the blanket."

Mother bowed her head with a sigh, a hand against her brow.

"Stay right where you are, Bonnie. I'm going to get something from the medicine cabinet."

"I'm not sick, Mom. I just itch," I said when she returned with a clear container of pink liquid.

"I realize you're not ill, dear."

"Then what's in the bottle you're opening?"

"It's called calamine lotion. Thanks to my mother, you have poison ivy. This will help with the discomfort. For now, try not to scratch. You'll only make it worse."

My beloved grandmother, I learned, was not allergic. I, on the other hand . . .

# Practice What You Preach

"Remember, dear, you must live by the words of Matthew 6, verse 33: "Seek first the kingdom of God and his righteousness, and all these things will be added to you."

My mother turned toward me, teeth clenched and shoulders tensed. Over the years, the stress of visits from her oldest sister, a Christian zealot, had become more evident.

I don't recollect what faith my aunt claimed as the one-and-only, but profess it she did. Immediately upon arrival. Loud and clear. It peeved my mom to be preached to and handed numerous little God pamphlets. Mother had a strong faith, evident in her words and actions. Unlike her sister, however, she did not judge others on theirs or lack thereof.

Aside from my aunt's presumptuous piousness, she had a rather pleasant personality. My mom, being the youngest of eight children born to her own mother and not having grown up with her older half-sibling, was just happy for the visits and tried to be tolerant and accepting.

Mother's forbearance, however, eventually proved limited in one regard. Each time my affluent aunt came to visit, she would bring me and my little sister a present. It wasn't the fact we received unearned acknowledgement that irritated my mother but that my brother did not.

After a few years of allowing this obvious female favoritism, Mother lost patience. With a tad of religious retaliation she told her sister, "I disapprove of your not treating the children equally, which would be the fair and Christian thing to do. I think you need to pray about this before you decide to bring any more gifts for the girls."

I don't know what the Lord answered, but I do know there were no more presents.

# Best Friends

"Can I ride with, Mom?"

"Well, if you like. But we trust you at home with your brother, you know."

"Yes, but I want to come."

I enjoyed visiting my mother's best friend. She let me do little chores and always had a compliment for me afterward. The two met while working at Honeywell after the war. Over the years, her husband became my dad's closest friend and ally.

We often went to see them in their tiny house in Ramsey. Sometimes I sat in the living room and played with my sister while they chatted. More often I asked to go to the basement where I spent an hour or so sweeping the floor and straightening the pantry, coming upstairs now and again under the guise of needing further direction.

I had an agenda, you see. I wanted to witness the inconceivable event that always played out at the kitchen table. Traversing the basement steps allowed me the opportunity.

When my dad, who was vexed by any audible eating noises, sat with his best friend, Emily Post's book of etiquette flew right out the window. (Excuse my cliché but it's exactly the image that comes to mind.)

The two of them would pop open a beer, pull out a package of Mallomars and eat, chat and smack for an hour or more. Yes, you heard correctly. Smack. Oh, not my father. Heavens, no. But his best buddy could make more noise with his mouth than could be generated with the aggressive use of a toilet plunger, I swear!

I marveled at Dad's self-control. There was never an angry glare nor unkind word. His show of restraint was, for me, a lesson unspoken.

My hard-working father had not the time to cultivate a plethora of friends; but for the ones he treasured, the gravest of infractions could be overlooked.

# One for the Record Books

"**W**ho do you think your folks are going to vote for?"

"Not for any Catholic, that's for sure!"

"How about you, Bonnie? Are your parents Republicans or Democrats?"

"I have no idea," I said.

As I walked away, the playground prattle dimmed.

I'd just started sixth grade the fall of 1960 when incumbent vice president Richard Nixon ran against John F. Kennedy for the highest office in the land.

I did not know nor would I have asked to which party my parents held allegiance. It was a private matter, even between the two of them.

They were not immune, however, to the contentious issues of the day. During the months leading up to the election, I caught snippets of conversations. A couple of things seemed concerning and neither had any relationship to party platform.

Age appeared to be a significant factor. Senator Kennedy was only forty-three. Of greater importance, at least to my mother, was religion. If he were to be the people's choice, he would not only become the youngest elected to the office of President of the United States but also the first Roman Catholic to hold the title.

It ended up a close race, one both notable and controversial, making history for reasons beyond age and faith. To this day, I know not for whom my parents cast their ballot.

I do, however, remember they always listened with reverence and respect every time the eloquent young man from Massachusetts stood behind a microphone.

# She Was the Bomb

My sixth grade teacher (whose name, for obvious reasons, I will not spell out) had a surname ending in the sound bēē, but when talking about her — not within earshot, of course — we students would often pronounce it as bomb. Kids can be cruel, but, truth be told, she was the mean one.

Back then, classroom climate was different. Instructors were revered and had broad authority to punish in whatever fashion suited them. Parents were supportive.

My folks always said, "Remember, if you get in trouble at school the penalty will be worse at home." In some cases, it was a good thing. Concerning this teacher, it was not.

Her problem: She did not like boys. No, let me rephrase. She *detested* boys.

One memorable morning we girls were removed from the classroom and shown a movie explaining our "monthly" (as it was delicately referred to). Upon returning to class, we were greeted by the snickering of every immature male in the room.

Without warning, a frequent troublemaker grabbed for a girl's informational pamphlet. The teacher spotted his misconduct. Man, did she light into him!

First came the painful, ruler-across-the-knuckles punishment. Then she handed him a dress to slip over his clothes and told him to stand in the open closet at the back of the room. He remained there until lunchtime.

That was her typical punishment for mischievous males. I thought it degrading, humiliating, unkind and undeserved, regardless the classroom infraction.

Girls were punished seldom and never in a manner to cause physical or emotional harm. Even so, at sixth-grade graduation, we were all, boys and girls alike, delighted to leave the "bomb" behind.

# Trick-or-Treat

My parents' philosophy regarding Halloween mirrored that of birthdays. No big deal.

Mother used her sewing talent to create costumes from household discards so we kids had something to wear for the obligatory elementary-school hallway "parade." But there was no evening trick-or-treating. They considered it senseless to gather a stockpile of junk food which served only to rot our teeth.

After school, we found a few treats from Mom and Dad. Usually a couple of Hershey's Milk-Chocolate candy bars (oh, how I savored each little square) and maybe some Pixy Stix or a package of M & M's. If a bag of Circus Peanuts complemented the offerings, we knew Dad had helped with the shopping. Those were his favorites.

One particular Halloween, however, stands out in my memory. I'd started sixth grade, the last level in our elementary building, and Mom said I could sleep overnight at the home of a classmate who lived near the school.

While chatting on the playground, some of the other girls learned of the plan to stay at my friend's house. One of them asked what we were going to do for Halloween. Most considered themselves too old for trick or treating. But when they learned I'd never been, a strategy formulated.

As the sun set, those who lived nearby met outside the front entrance of the school building. Each had painted or smudged their face to assure anonymity and used whatever could be found to create a makeshift costume.

One dressed as a vampire, all in black, with blood (lipstick) dripping from her chin and another a ghost, her identity concealed with a threadbare sheet, holes cut for the eyes. I donned a ragged sweatshirt and dirty ball cap, both donated by my friend's older brother, and carried a stuffed kerchief tied to a stick slung over my shoulder.

I don't recall whether we amassed any candy. I do remember the thrill of being out with girlfriends running the neighborhood, whooping and hollering like a little kid, having the time of my life!

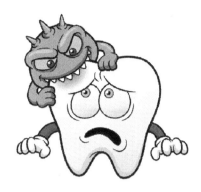

# A "Sticky" Subject

"If you don't get it out soon, your permanent one is going to come in behind the baby tooth just like a few others have done."

"Oh, Mom, you know how I hate wiggling loose teeth. The feeling is so weird and the taste of blood in my mouth makes me want to barf."

"You're so dramatic, Bonnie. I guess you could wait for your dad to get home. He'd make quick work of it."

I hated the ongoing torture of tooth removal. I didn't understand why they couldn't all just fall out at the same time. The fickle, fang fairy could have slipped a crisp Washington under my pillow and it would not have altered my feelings.

Some fell out on their own, and I know for a fact one or two went down my throat during the night. (I don't have to tell you how I know this.) But as I neared sixth grade graduation, when most kids had lost all their milk teeth, I held firm to three.

Then one spring afternoon, the teacher sent us home with a notice from the PTA indicating they'd be going room to room the next day selling popcorn balls. Students were to bring a dime for each one they wanted to purchase.

The next day I handed over thirty cents, slipped one each for my brother and sister into my book bag, and took mine outside to enjoy during recess.

With the first mouthful, I felt an unusual crunch. It was not a popcorn kernel. I'd lost a tooth! I stuffed it in my pocket and, with focused determination, took another large bite.

To my delight and amazement — since it involved no wiggling, blood or string — that sticky orb caused the final demise of all my remaining deciduous teeth.

# Personal Preference

"Mom, are you in there?"

"Yes, dear, and I'll be a while longer."

"The bus'll come in five minutes, Mom, and I haven't brushed my teeth yet!"

"Well, Bonnie, you know what they say, 'bad planning on your part does not constitute an emergency on mine.'"

She was right. I had not allocated my time properly. On most school days, as a matter of habit, I would brush my teeth right after breakfast, before my brother took a quarter of an hour to slick back his hair or Mother settled in for her morning ritual.

It was due to an error in judgement the night before. While I was doing homework, my brother, in an uncharacteristic gesture of generosity, asked if I wanted to borrow his new transistor radio for a while. *Of course, I did.* But while I swooned to Neil Sedaka's Stairway to Heaven, my math homework went undone.

So there I stood, in quite the morning pickle. I'd spent a precious ten minutes finishing my arithmetic assignment when I should have been coiffing my curls and tending my teeth — a mistake I regretted.

"I know it's my fault, Mom, but can't you hurry? Please?"

"No, I cannot. But there's room for two in here. Remember, if you miss the bus, you'll be walking to school."

There it was. I had no choice.

Entering, I tried not to look. I tried harder not to inhale. I was successful at neither. It was a scarring experience, one which left me with a lifelong preference for private bathroom time.

# Sandbox Shenanigans

"I'll take the little bucket and fill it from the hose. Then we'll make a castle if you want."

"Oh, yes," she gushed. "I love castles!"

Our old sandbox was nothing more than a discarded tire from a G series Minneapolis-Moline tractor. For me it lost its appeal when my brother no longer felt the desire to dig in the dirt with his younger female cohort.

But when my sister got old enough, I once again enjoyed sitting on the tire's edge helping her make simple sand creations and reliving the pleasures of a younger childhood. She could be entertained for hours with a few discarded Tupperware containers, an old metal spoon and a vivid imagination.

It was her favorite place.

Then one fateful morning, after I found my white rat, Pixie, a red-eyed rodent my young sibling had grown quite attached to, dead in her cage, my mother demanded, "Bonnie, go bury that animal someplace your sister will never find it!"

In thoughtless haste, since I didn't want to miss the bus and have to walk to school, I dug a shallow grave and disposed of my expired pet in the sand.

Yes, the sand of the first place my little sis went to play that morning.

Upon returning home, I was greeted by a scathing look from Mother and the well-deserved punishment of a week's worth of extra chores.

# Rub-a-Dub Dispensation

"**I**'m first."

"No, you're not. You snuck in before me last week."

"I did not."

"Yes, you did!"

"Mom, tell him it's my turn, please!"

"Your brother's right, Bonnie. You were first in the tub last time. It's his turn tonight."

"Aw, jeez! I hate taking a bath in his leftover boy scum."

"Oh, stop complaining. It's not the end of the world. You can run a little more hot to warm it up when you get in."

For years that's how the conversation had gone most Saturday nights around our house.

Given the fact we had a well and septic system, $H_2O$ was something everyone in our family learned to consume only in amounts absolutely necessary.

Brushing my teeth meant using a small cup in which to dip and rinse my toothbrush versus letting the faucet run. And, as far as toilet etiquette, we adhered to the disgusting practice alluded to in the phrase, "If it's yellow, let it mellow; if ..."

But what I disliked the most was bath rationing. Not only were we restricted to an amount of liquid barely sufficient to cover one's bum, we also had to reuse.

Then came puberty; and, though, for a girl, reaching a certain age of maturity brought some negatives, it also provided one significant positive. I was no longer required to share my bath water.

# Shoo Fly

"Come on. Let's slip under the fence and play in the pasture," he said.

"No, I have a good shirt on, and I don't want to catch it on a barb," I whined.

"Oh, come on, Sis. Don't be such a baby. We'll each hold the wire for the other so there'll be plenty of room to scoot under."

Whenever we visited our maternal grandmother, there were lots of fun things to do. We took turns pushing each other in the tire swing overlooking her massive iris garden, snooped in some of the many dilapidated out buildings, or rode our bikes round and round the expansive circle driveway.

This particular visit, we decided to go exploring in the woods behind the house. Part of the fenced-in area was pasture for a dozen or so cows and the rest, rolling hills and a few wetlands.

After successful how-low-can-you-go belly crawls, we ran to a place called the gravel pit and pocketed a few pretty agates. Then my brother decided we should follow the fence line to see just how far Grandma's property extended.

As we entered a low area puddled from a recent rain, something strange came into view.

"What do you suppose it is?" he asked.

"I don't know, but it sure is big."

By then, we'd walked close enough to identify the object: a cow. A dead cow. The young animal had met with an untimely demise and its stomach had bloated up like a hot air balloon ready to lift off. And, oh my Lord, the odor!

"Come on, let's get out of here," he coughed with a hand over his nose.

But I'd picked up a sturdy, long stick and was ready to quench a curiosity.

"No, wait a second," I said as the wood made contact with one gargantuan cow gut.

Before I could pull back and toss the stick, we were bombarded by thousands of maggot flies. It felt like a scene from a horror flick.

Screaming and flailing our arms we sprinted back to our original entry point. This time we slid under with haste and without the slightest concern of a snag.

# Feed a Moose a Marshmallow

"Hey, your stupid horse is chewing on his stall again."

"Stop calling him stupid. He's not."

"Well, any horse only willing to rein in one direction is pretty dumb in my book. And he's proving it by chomping on wood. What's his problem, anyway?"

"He doesn't have a problem. You do. You're just being mean."

"No, I'm being honest. That big sorrel gelding is minus a brain. I think they removed it with some other parts."

"Oh, and I suppose your skinny stallion is some sort of intellectual genius."

"Well, at least he has enough sense to know wood isn't something to consume."

"My Moose may not be the smartest, but he's a whole lot gentler than your uppity Charlie Horse."

"Okay, Charlie's a bit high-strung, but he knows what he is and isn't supposed to eat."

"Well, maybe Moose is just bored with the taste of hay and grain. Hmm, didn't Mom say she was planning to make Rice Krispies Treats today?"

"I think so, why?"

"Never mind. I'll be right back."

"What are you going to do?" he kept yelling as I hurried to the back door, entered the kitchen, grabbed from the bag on the counter and ran back to the barn.

"Look," I said, opening my hand. "I'm going to see if Moose wants a bit of a treat."

"Marshmallows? Are you nuts! No self-respecting horse is going to eat a marshmallow."

Paying no attention, I extended my arm, palm up offering the gummy goodness to my trusty steed.

A spray of snot covered my wrist as wet nostrils sniffed the unusual offering. Then, to our surprise, his upper lip shot out and engulfed the two puff balls.

We collapsed in a fit of laughter watching the idiotic antics of my silly horse — his jaw snapping up and down and tongue flapping in and out, attempting to masticate those minuscule morsels.

*Maybe my brother was onto something?*

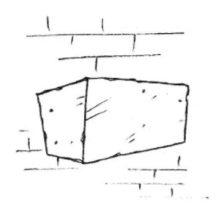

# The "Yellow Brick Road"

W ell, in truth it wasn't yellow, nor a road.

A line of cement blocks ran parallel to our driveway, graduated in height from tallest at the sidewalk to lowest where the front yard ended. It originated as a barrier to hold fill and black dirt brought in to level the ground before seeding.

The wall became a favorite place to play. Blocks had been laid one on top of another with holes up. Maybe there'd been a thought to add something decorative to the top surface, but it never happened.

The placement, however, created a type of avoidance balance beam. We enjoyed challenging each other to see who could run the wall fastest without catching a foot in the process — harder than it sounds.

Those openings also made convenient places to hide things, whether a half-eaten apple to assure Mother's ignorance of my wastefulness or the faded and peeling hair barrette I "lost" at school.

With help from the brick wall, I learned to balance on my two-wheeler. The first time I released from its safety and took off down the driveway was a moment of pride. Until the need to stop, that is. As I recall, much blood and a substantial amount of mercurochrome followed.

The wall later served as a leg-up to mount my steed. Guiding Moose close enough was difficult and persuading him to remain still while I stuck a foot in the stirrup, even more arduous. On one occasion, my gentle giant of a horse, just as my foot neared the stirrup, took off lickety-split for the barn. I found him with his nose in the grain bin. There was no coaxing him back to the wall.

Granted, it was simply a bulwark of builder-grade blocks, but our "yellow brick road" led to many a memorable childhood adventure.

# A Shocker!

"What in the name of heaven are you two doing out here? You're making enough noise to wake the dead," she said, as her eyes darted from us to the disturbing sight at the corner of the house.

My brother and I were having our usual contest to see who could toss a basketball up and over the house. As we laughed and taunted each other, the ball rolled back down our side of the roof and smack dab into Mother's prized garden of tiger lilies.

At that exact moment Mom exited the back door.

"Look what you've done," she continued. "Half my flower garden is flattened!"

"Sorry, Mom," we said, heads hung.

"Well, I'm going to send your sister out," she announced with a frown."I have things to do in the house. You two can watch her for an hour or so, and I'd appreciate your playing something a bit less rowdy and destructive.

"By the way, your father said to remind you to clean the barn this afternoon and be sure to check the electric fence some time today."

"Yes, Mom," we answered in unison.

Neither of us enjoyed the task of cleaning the barn; and our sister, not yet five years old, was too little to be of help. But the job came with the privilege of having horses. Thus, every Saturday, we took up pitchforks and a wheelbarrow. And while our eyes watered and nostrils burned from the malodorous mixture of feces and ammonia, we dutifully removed a week's worth horse hockey, donkey dung and urine-soaked straw.

So when Mother sent our young sibling outside, my mischievous brother, in a misguided attempt to include her in the day's workload, whispered to me with a slight tone of sadistic delight, "I think we should have her test the electric fence."

It was a simple matter of licking the end of one's finger and touching the top wire, resulting in more of a sizzle than much of a shock. But, alas, in her excitement to help, the little tyke grabbed the wire with her entire tiny fist and could not let go.

We exchanged looks of terror before my brother, resembling a modern-day Flash, sprinted to the barn and threw the breaker controlling juice to the fence.

I don't remember what sort of bargain we struck that day, but our little sis didn't tattle on us. And we never did anything so mean to her again. Well, maybe . . .

# Better to Give

"Remember, you two, it's important to keep her away from the barn. Your mother and I want this to be a surprise. We're counting on you both."

It was December, 1961, and my horse-loving little sister had just turned five. Being too small to ride our mounts, Mom and Dad decided to get her a pony of her own.

So two days before Christmas, an aging and docile Shetland named Butterball had been covertly stashed in our barn. My brother and I were tasked with keeping the secret and making sure our precocious sibling stayed far away from the horse stalls.

A snowy, cold winter in Minnesota had left a foot of white stuff on the ground, so we managed to keep our sister busy inside with games and coloring books. With rare camaraderie, we executed our assignment in a spirit of eager excitement and delightful deception.

Everyone except my father attended candlelight services Christmas Eve. While we raised our voices in holiday harmony, Dad kept busy in the barn brushing even the smallest dirt clumps from the thick winter coat of little Butterball and combing out the countless tangles from his long, multi-colored mane and tail.

After an overnight snowfall, Christmas morning dawned crisp, clear and full of all the usual childhood delight. As the three of us gathered under the tinsel-draped tree opening the last of our presents, our father escaped unnoticed from the house.

A few minutes later, we heard a tap, tap, tap on the living room picture window. There stood Dad in the glittering, new-fallen snow holding the halter of a plump and primped, brown and white pony with a bright red bow circling its chubby neck.

The expression of jubilation on my sister's face brought me more pleasure than any gift under the tree. At that moment, I realized the true benefit of giving over receiving.

# Those Pesky Pigeons

"Scram, you feathered fiends," he shouted while stabbing the atmosphere with his favorite, pronged instrument of attack.

Dad was in one of his "fowl" moods again. I knew to keep my distance and hold my tongue.

"Don't just stand there, Bonnie," he scolded. "Go turn on the water and bring me the end of the hose."

I ran to the outside faucet and, after clearing earshot, let loose a snicker of delightful anticipation. I knew what came next. It had become a regular back-yard caper.

The rear wall of the addition to our house, due to Dad's propensity to procrastinate, had been left bare of siding. Finished only to the point of weather-tight, there remained, for years, a single layer of tar paper to take the impact of the elements.

And, for reasons beyond our understanding, pigeons loved to roost on the eaves and poop down the sticky black surface. They came in flocks and congregated by the dozens for hours at a time.

More than persistent, they seemed to exude intent — perched with beaks to the peak and tail feathers twisting in the wind. The excrement created a disgusting mess of whitish "plaster" impervious to the most pelting of rainstorms.

Dad tried everything possible to discourage them. His antics with hosepipe and pitchfork made me laugh but did little to deter those determined birds.

# Cover Your Eyes, Miss Manners

"Mom, is it okay if I walk over to Uncle's place for a while?"

"That's fine, Bonnie, but remember it's been a wet spring. There'll be lots of poison ivy along the edges of his driveway."

"Don't worry. I'll walk right down the middle!"

"When you get there, would you let him know I'll drive over after I visit a while longer with Mother?"

"Sure, I'll tell him. Bye, Grandma."

"Goodbye, Bonnie. See you next time."

After Grandpa passed, my mother's oldest brother took up residence in the little shack in the woods situated on one of the two forty-acre plots across the road from Grandma.

He was a lifelong bachelor, but he loved kids and I cherished our visits together. We might stroll through the woods to admire a blooming lady's slipper or work up a sweat stacking cordwood. Whatever the adventure, the best part was taking a break afterward.

In his gruff, booming voice he'd say to me, "I imagine you're as thirsty as I am. Why don't you go out to the garage and get yourself a pop. Grab me one too, would you?"

The old lean-to garage had a dirt floor and Uncle kept the customary two wooden cases of soda snuggled into the coolest corner. I'd grab a Grape Crush — my favorite — and an Orange — his — and run back to the cabin.

While I slugged that carbonated indulgence straight from the bottle (a rare treat to begin with and one I'd otherwise be required to imbibe in ladylike fashion from a glass), he'd pull out a package of Fig Newtons. I was not a fan and less so after he told me the filling had a grainy texture because they made it from what the factory workers scraped off their boots. Over the years I realized this to be nothing more than an uncle untruth intended to discourage me from devouring his favorite fig-filled confections.

But *my* ultimate treat waited on the top shelf above his tiny table. He'd grab it down and set the jar and a table knife in front of me. Once again, I would break the rules of etiquette, dip deep into the depths of Skippy deliciousness and indulge myself — directly from the blade!

As I neared the end of the long driveway, I saw Uncle exit the cabin with a shot gun slung over his shoulder.

"Hey there, Bonnie," he said. "Good to see you. Where's your Ma?"

"She'll be over later. She wants to talk with Grandma for a while yet."

"Well, I was just headed through the woods to the lake. I need to check my beaver traps. It won't take long. Would you like to come?"

"You bet!"

As we approached the area near the snares, dampness seeped through my tennis shoes and soaked my cotton socks. I didn't care. Time with my uncle eclipsed any negatives.

Upon our return, unfortunately empty-handed, he said, "Well, that didn't take very long at all, Bonnie. Why don't you fetch us some liquid refreshment from the garage and meet me in the cabin for our usual snack."

A half-hour later, hearing Mother's car crunching up the gravel driveway, Uncle shot me a sly wink, tossed the evidence into the tin wash basin atop the wood stove and replaced the infamous jar of peanut-y pleasure.

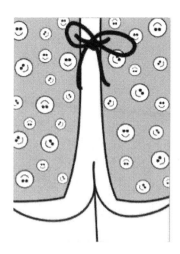

# Exposed!

"Come on girls. Get a move on. Three laps around the room to start."

We listened to the same mantra every day as our instructor strolled the locker room demanding haste as we changed into our faded, one-piece button-front gym suits. I didn't like her, and I hated Phys Ed. Unfortunately, it was a necessary evil of junior high.

Physical fitness of any type was difficult since my weight always tipped a tad toward the bulky side. And it was made more arduous by the fact I had not been blessed with even a modicum of innate talent for any organized sport, though I'd been known to dunk a basketball once or twice.

And when the curriculum cycled to the tumbling unit, well, I'll just be honest. If my current ancestry.com account discovered a distant DNA link to Cathy Rigby, I'm certain she would contest its accuracy. I was a total loser.

I understood the importance of introducing young people to a variety of physical activities. What I didn't fathom, however, was the need to expose our fragile, pubescent egos to an even greater degree of humiliation in the form of the requisite gang shower.

"Hurry up, ladies. You've got five minutes to shower and change before the bell rings," she reminded at the end of class as her eyes traveled up and down the rows of young women in various stages of undress, clothing piled on benches or tossed into open lockers.

"Come on, lose the towel," she scolded as I approached the entrance of the shower room. Then, with a glint in her eye and a look I could only describe as perverse pleasure, she grabbed the tucked-in corner of my too-tiny towel and gave a firm tug, leaving me, well, you know.

It's possible she "liked" us way more than we cared for her.

# A Bit of Daddy Deception

"I see your mother's outside hanging laundry, Bonnie. Why don't you get a paper cup from the kitchen and I'll share with you."

We'd just come in from barn chores. Since my brother was working his first summer part-time job, I wielded the pitchfork alone to muck out the stalls that day. Dad took charge of the wheelbarrow, pushing each load to the manure pile. We were hot, exhausted and in need of a cold beverage.

Mother, who frowned upon the intake of alcohol, would, on occasion, allow Dad to buy a six-pack of beer. I watched them unload groceries the day before, and was thrilled for what I knew, from past experience, came next.

My father and I shared few adventures. He was either working hard or resting from doing so. And, to be honest, interacting with children wasn't really his strength. So this collusion and camaraderie became equal in excitement to the underage taste of that frothy, golden-hued libation.

When I returned from the kitchen, cup in hand, Dad shared enough for two big gulps. I chose tiny sips to make the experience, with both my father and the forbidden beverage, last as long as possible.

"Remember, this is our little secret, right?" he reminded.

After motioning the zipping of my lips, I replied, "I won't say a word, Dad, I promise."

It's possible Mom knew of our covert conspiracy, but she never let on.

# "Holy" Hosiery!

"Why do I have to wear these, Mom?"

"Because you're starting high school in the fall. It's time you switched from socks to nylons, at least for special occasions like this. I'm sure the other girls will be wearing them. You don't want to look out of place, do you?"

"I've tried to get them on already. It's not worth it. I don't care if I stick out."

"Come now, Bonnie. You're making it worse than it is. Remember, you're the one who refuses to wear a garter belt, and this is the latest fashion alternative. So settle down a bit and have another go at it. I'll help if you want."

"Good grief, no. I don't need my mother's help!"

"Well, okay then. I offered. Remember, we have to be at church in an hour for a group photo before the service, so you don't have all morning to figure this out. And try to be gentle, dear. It's not like yanking on your barn boots."

Once again, I gathered the material of one leg. Moving with cautious determination, I slipped my right foot through the scrunched up nylon down to the reinforced toe. Then a rough spot on my heel caught in the threads. I freed it with a slight tug and proceeded with the left leg.

Thinking I'd won a victory in the battle of the panty hose, I stood and adjusted them to my waist. Before announcing my success, I turned to admire my reflection in the full-length mirror on the back of my door. The suntan color of nylon was interrupted by the white of skin glaring through a wide path leading from heel to calf and beyond.

After angrily removing and disposing of the infuriating leg wear, I pulled on my usual foot covering, slipped on black flats and presented myself to Mom.

With a sigh and a smile of resignation, she said, "You look very pretty, Bonnie. Go get in the car. It's time to leave."

I smoothed my cotton broadcloth dress beneath me with care as I slid onto the back seat next to my siblings. A few creases in my skirt, however, ended up an insignificant concern.

Of the fifteen girls who lined up in front of the boys that day for our ninth grade confirmation class photo, only I sported bobby socks.

# Back in the Saddle

"**I** was so scared, Mom. I thought for sure we were going to be killed!"

"Oh honey, I'm so thankful you're okay," she said, with arms around me in a rare embrace and a softness in her voice I seldom heard.

I had been enjoying a horseback ride and decided to cross the highway to visit a friend. It wasn't the first time I took Moose across, and I had no reason to expect a problem.

As I urged him onto the blacktop, a semi truck and trailer came barreling down the pavement, horn blasting. For whatever reason — noise or vibration — my unshakable horse reared up with a diesel giant headed straight for us.

I held tight and attempted to rein Moose away from the oncoming danger. In my haste, however, I forgot one important fact about my steady steed. Having come from a riding stable, he balked at turning the opposite direction from what he was accustomed.

In those seconds of hesitation, I felt sure we were destined to become fresh roadkill. Suddenly, Moose stepped back off the asphalt. The big rig flew past. I trembled in the saddle, angry at my horse and embarrassed by my lack of composure.

As Mom and I sat snuggled together on the edge of the bed, she listened with patience and understanding while I sobbed through the telling.

Then she straightened and, in her more standard suck-it-up-and-get-on-with-it tone, stated, "Well, Bonnie, I think you and your horse share the blame for this one. You can't let one unpleasant incident keep you from something you enjoy. So get back out there and mount up."

# I Like Happy Endings

"Once upon a time, a young, golden-haired girl dreamed of being a princess in a castle. She imagined having a room of her own and dozens of books about people in exotic, far-off places," I said, beginning our shared, fanciful nighttime narrative.

"But the little girl didn't have a daddy," my sister added, "and lived in a tiny house with her mom and six older brothers and sisters."

"Yes," I said, "the family was so poor sometimes all they had to eat for dinner was warm milk and crackers."

"And all three of the girls had to sleep in the same bed."

That's the way we began our bedtime ritual. Her on the top bunk, me on the bottom, bridging an age gap with our imaginations. I don't remember how the back-and-forth storytelling tradition started. Likely it sprung from a need to mask the scary noises emanating from the dense woods that had become our second home.

After my uncle moved into my grandfather's old place in the woods, my parents purchased the adjoining, undeveloped forty acres from Grandma. A few years later, when we finished clearing land for a driveway, our family became seasonal residents.

The first summer, we kids slept on the floor of the tiny mobile home Mom and Dad bought and placed on their new property. It was close quarters for five; and Dad soon went to work building two small cabins, one for us girls and another for my brother.

So the following year, we lived in our own private little "castle." Dad found bunk beds to fit snuggly into one end of the 7 x 8 foot building; and Mother sewed red and white, gingham curtains for the two small windows. We had a couple of low benches, and, in one corner, a hand-made cupboard with a hinged door, chock-full of Mother's kitchen cast-offs.

The small building was situated a short sprint from the outhouse and very close to the tire swing Dad managed to attach to a high, sizable branch of the towering oak tree which cast afternoon shade on our little abode. It was all quite cozy.

"One very special evening," I continued with a tone of anticipation, "the girl's mother brought a man home to meet all her children. At first the little girl was shy around the visitor, but when he surprised her with a copy of Treasure Island, she decided it was okay for him to hang around."

There was a long pause. My sister loved our fictitious tale-telling, but she was weary from the day's outdoor activities.

"Are you still awake?" I whispered.

Her sleepy reply came in the form of an abrupt conclusion.

"The mother fell in love with the kind man," she yawned. "They got married and bought a huge house in a beautiful neighborhood. The little girl had her own private, pretty pink room filled with lots and lots of books about famous people and thrilling adventures.

"And they all lived happily ever after."

# A Numbers Nightmare

"I have a note from my math teacher for you, Mom."

"Oh? Did you get in some sort of trouble, Bonnie?"

"No, nothing like that."

"Well, let me see it then."

I handed her the paper. I had talked with the teacher and knew what it said. My fate was sealed.

"This tells me you're failing Modern Geometry."

"Yes, Mom."

"Well, I know you do your homework every night. You're not causing a disruption in class, are you?"

"No, Mom. You know I wouldn't."

"What seems to be the problem then?"

"It's just so hard. I don't get it at all."

"Hmm, I know your father and I aren't much help, but couldn't you stay after school a few nights and get some one-on-one time with the teacher?"

"He doesn't think it would be helpful."

"Why not? Sounds like he's trying to get out of doing his job."

"You haven't read the whole thing, Mom."

"Okay, let me see here." She paused to read the final paragraph.

"Oh my, he's suggesting you attend an evening adult education class relating to the foundations of modern math. But why would you need to do that?"

"Well, I'm struggling with the concept of modern geometry because I never had any classes in junior high using the new 'modern' way of learning math. Now as a sophomore, that's what I'm stuck with. And without some basic understanding, the method we're required to use makes no sense to me."

"Sounds logical, I guess. I'll talk with your father tonight, and we'll send a message back to your teacher tomorrow."

So the following week found me in a night class with an eclectic bunch of adults — them attempting to absorb enough to assist with their children's homework and me trying to stay afloat in hopeful anticipation of being allowed to disembark the vessel of high school with the rest of my class of '67.

Little did I know at the outset how much fun I'd have with those clueless "old people." They were such a hoot. I was almost sad when the eight-week class ended. And I don't think a one of them gleaned much knowledge from the class. I know I didn't.

But, lucky for me, since I exhibited the initiative and attended faithfully, I passed Modern Geometry with a solid D.

# My "Friend"

"Mom, that was Tammy on the line."

"Yes, I heard the telephone ring. But who's Tammy?"

"She's the girl I met at canoe camp in June. Don't you remember me talking about her and how much fun we had? She wanted to know if I could take the bus into Minneapolis tomorrow and meet her at the library. Afterward we could have lunch and maybe spend a little time shopping. I said I'd call her back after I talked to you."

"I'm not sure, Bonnie. To be honest, I don't feel good about you spending the day with someone you barely know."

"It *was* a ten-day canoe trip, Mom. I think we got to know each other pretty well. She's a nice person. But if you're concerned, why don't you call and talk with her parents?"

"No, that won't be necessary. Your father and I trust you, and you're old enough to use your own good judgement. If you're comfortable with the idea and want to go, it's fine. But you need to be home by supper time, so plan your bus schedule accordingly."

"Thanks, Mom. I'll call her back and set a time to meet."

I took the 8:00 a.m. bus the next morning and arrived at 8:45. I was not only excited to see my friend again but also looking forward to spending time in one of my favorite places. The new downtown library included a planetarium, the perfect place to relax under a darkened dome and watch the constellations twinkle.

During the first few minutes of our meeting, however, it became obvious Tammy's interests did not include star gazing. She came with one thought in mind: new school clothes.

I didn't care much for shopping, but I wanted my friend to be happy. So off we went to Dayton's.

As we walked aisle to aisle, Tammy seemed oblivious to my presence. So while she browsed the long bin of colorful scarves, I left her side to look elsewhere. She paid no heed to my absence.

Suddenly, on either side of me, appeared two store security guards. The man on my left stated, "We need you and your friend to come with us to the office."

My eyes pleaded for an explanation. Dampness stained my armpits.

Seeing my obvious distress, he assured, "Don't worry, *you* did nothing wrong."

During the hour-long interrogation, both the police and our parents were called. I learned Tammy had stuffed three scarves in her purse and intended to leave without paying for them. We'd both been under store surveillance, so they knew I was blameless.

The whole incident was mortifying. I felt used and manipulated. My "friend" had stolen something far more valuable than clothing accessories.

On the ride home, my father, with a firm yet understanding voice, said, "Well, Bonnie, I feel no need to scold you further. You've suffered enough and, in addition, I think you learned a valuable lesson today."

He was right.

# Rebellion Gone Awry

"It's going to get down below freezing tonight, ladies," Mother warned. "After we build up the fire, and even if you don't feel an immediate need, I suggest you make a trip to the outhouse before settling in."

Mom had been my Girl Scout troop leader for over ten years. She loved young people, and they returned the affection. As a Brownie, I'd been guilty of jealousy when she'd given individual attention to other troop members. It strained an already fragile middle-child ego.

Over the years, those feelings of envy dissipated. Unfortunately, for Mom, they were, on occasion, replaced with the typical I-know-everything-and-you-know-nothing attitude of adolescence. I could be contrary.

As juniors in high school, she was now subjecting our troop to the "adventure" of winter camping, an activity to complete the requirements for a coveted badge. Twelve of us would spend the night snuggled together in refrigerator boxes, six feet long and three feet wide: two to a box.

After turns in the latrine, it was time to bed down when Mother shouted one more command. "Remember, girls, even though it's already a tight squeeze, be sure to take your boots into the box with you. If you leave them outside, they'll be frozen in the morning."

I turned to my confined-in-cardboard companion who'd already complied and proclaimed, "Really? I don't believe that for a minute!"

Well, let me tell you. A rubber boot can freeze pretty darn solid. So while everyone else was enjoying a hot breakfast around the crackling campfire, I was huddled in my corrugated hut humbly hugging my frozen footwear.

# What a Rule-Breaker

"Be sure you bring her up right at seven o'clock. That's when all the meal trays will be taken away and there won't be many people in the hall."

"Yes, dear, I remember," my father answered in a tone of obedience. "Bonnie can come sit with you like she did before. We'll stay downstairs in the main lounge until the 'appointed' hour."

Mom underwent her radical mastectomy surgery during an era when children under a certain age were not allowed to see loved ones in the hospital.

My strong-willed mother, however, would not be denied a visit by her youngest child. So she and my dad devised a plan.

Since Mom was at the end of the hall, closest to the emergency exit (and I wouldn't put it past her to have requested that room), Dad would wait until the hallways were calm and sneak my sister up the staircase.

Only once did they get caught breaking the rules.

The kind and understanding nurse, however, must have been a mother herself. She smiled, cautioned with "just five more minutes," and closed the door behind her.

# No Big Heads, Please

In regard to educational expectations, my parents went by a simple rule: Respect your teachers, always give your best effort and be modest in your accomplishments.

It served as subtle encouragement, yet allowed for the occasional screw up. I tended to be an obedient student and though not the brainiest kid in school neither was I a slouch.

During my junior year, I doubled my efforts, and working my mental muscles paid off. When I received my year-end report card, I glanced down the column to see four A's and two B's. I was elated and eager to share my awesome news with Mother.

Bounding in the door, I found her at the ironing board.

"Mom, I got my grades today."

"Well, you seem happy enough. I trust there are no D's on it this time."

"Nope. Not a one," I said with a grin.

Mom placed the iron back on its heat source and said, "Well, how about you show me what you appear so proud of."

I handed her the folded paper.

"Hmm, looks like you finished the year with some good marks."

"Isn't it cool, Mom? I got four A's. That's the best I've ever done in high school. I'll be on the Honor Roll and have my name in the paper and everything!"

Not one to be demonstrative nor overly complimentary, my mother replied with a simple acknowledgment cloaked in a demand for humility.

"Yes, you did well, Bonnie. You deserve to be proud. But remember, don't start thinking you're better than anyone else."

# Sibling Sendoff

"Why do you have to go again?"

"I need to fight the commies," he answered with bravado. "Don't you get it? It's the right thing to do."

"Oh, I understand just fine. But it isn't the same around here without you."

"Maybe not, but at least you don't have to listen to Dad yell at me when I mess up."

"I don't care. I hate that you're being sent to that dangerous place. You could get hurt or even killed! Aren't you scared?"

"I've been training almost a year for this. I'm not afraid and you shouldn't be either. I do hope you'll write every week and keep me up on what's happening."

"Will you write back?"

"Well, I won't make any promises, but I'll try. It'll depend on where I'm stationed and what duties I'm assigned. Might be tough to write a letter from a rice paddy."

Throughout the tumultuous teenage years my brother's antics caused our parents a good many sleepless nights, but he and I shared secrets and kept each other's confidences. I'd overheard my Dad say the military would "be good for him" and "make him a man" but I'd not been at all keen on the idea, and even less so now.

"Don't worry, Bonnie, I'll be fine," he continued. "I'm sorry I'll miss your graduation, but I promise to send you something. While I'm gone, I want you to continue exercising Charlie Horse for me, and for heaven's sake keep a salt block in the pasture so that empty-headed equine of yours doesn't eat up the barn!"

"You're so mean," I said as I punched him in the arm. "I take it all back. I won't miss you one little bit!"

He put his arm around my shoulders and tears flooded my eyes.

"Yes, you will. And I'll miss you, too."

# Nature's Anomaly

I was a working girl in 1966. No, not a floozy on the street corner. Nothing so lucrative. I clerked at a five-and-dime. But I earned a dollar an hour, which seemed a fortune considering I made half that babysitting.

It was the summer before my senior year; and, since I had no car, I depended on my father for a ride to work. My job at the shopping center was a forty-five minute drive from our rustic summertime residence in a wooded area north of the Twin Cities, and Dad's an additional hour away. The distance involved made it necessary for us to leave at the ridiculous hour of four o'clock in the morning.

Our first pre-dawn drive together was a wet one. An overnight rainstorm had passed through and the roads were damp. I dozed as my father whizzed down the asphalt and around the many twists and turns of those dark country roads.

Then a peculiar noise brought me alert, a sound so unearthly it evaded human description. Our tires were creating a cacophony of juicy squishing and smooshing. While my dad explained the anomaly, it was all I could do to hold down the morning's cold strawberry Pop-Tart.

Remember the age-old phrase, "The early bird catches the worm?" Well, substitute "frog" for "bird" and you'll need no further elaboration.

After Dad dropped me at a friend's house, where I planned to sleep on the couch until she and I walked together to work, my memory kept replaying the abhorrent sound of amphibian annihilation.

And so it continued. Each morning after a rainfall, at the fateful turn where marshland flanked asphalt. Dozens of God's creations, small, green and helpless, met their fate via Firestone.

# One Banana, Two . . .

Growing up with parents who lived through the Great Depression and WWII, I heard the following phrases often:

"Use it up, wear it out, make it do or do without."

"Why buy new when slightly used will do."

"Reduce, reuse, recycle."

"Money doesn't grow on trees you know."

And my mother's favorite, "Live simply so others might simply live."

Those ideals and habits of conservation are as much a part of my beliefs and actions today as they are, I sense, an unconscious effort to honor my mother's legacy.

I know for a fact, however, she would not be pleased with my current-day approach to bananas. Yes, you read that right: bananas.

Growing up, there wasn't a great deal of fresh fruit in our house. Maybe apples, if Mom intended to bake a pie or cobbler; otherwise our fruit came from a can — the exception being bananas. Maybe they were Dad's favorites, I don't know. What I do know is we were allowed only a half with our breakfast.

"Nobody needs a whole banana," Mother would say. "Cut it in half and share with your dad or brother."

So even today when I reach for a banana with my morning cereal, I hear my mother's voice questioning, "Now, Bonnie, do you really need the entire thing, or would half do just fine?"

# "Crushed"

I admit to a junior-high infatuation with Maverick. Yes, I had a centerfold of James Garner taped to the inside of my locker. Laugh if you must, but I was quite smitten.

Though I never dated during high school, I did move on to a new flame. I remember every detail of our first meeting.

It was a Saturday morning. He was browsing in the women's-wear section. Maybe in his mid-twenties, the man was tall and boyishly handsome with an athletic build.

When he approached the checkout, a colorful lady's scarf in hand, he asked, "Could I have this gift-wrapped, please?"

I was, without a doubt, inept with paper and tape. But we offered the free service, and as an employee at the front counter I had no choice but to give it my best shot.

After choosing the right size box, I sliced from the large roll what I estimated to be an ample amount of paper, pulled the cellophane tape from a drawer and began.

I must have appeared as clueless and flustered as I felt because, in the kindest voice, he asked, "Would you like me to show you how to do that with as little waste as possible?"

As I stared into the abyss of his sapphire eyes, I stammered, "Uh, sure, I guess. I've never been very good at this."

"Well, there is a bit of a trick to it. Just watch and you'll see it's not at all difficult."

As he leaned over the counter to begin the process, I was hypnotized by the scent of Old Spice and entranced by the way his sandy brown hair brushed the top of perfect eyebrows.

Then, during his instruction on the best way to fold and tape the ends of the package, his hand brushed against my bare forearm. My cheeks warmed and my stomach fluttered.

"There," he said. "Now attach the bow and we're all set."

"Thank you," I answered. "I'll certainly be better prepared next time."

With an intoxicating smile, he said, "I look forward to it."

I stood there mute, experiencing an overwhelming desire to be the girl he purchased that scarf for and dreaming of the next time I'd see him.

A few weeks later, he came back. He was not alone.

When he approached the register, I smiled and said a shy, "Hello."

"Yes, hello again," he said.

*He remembered me! Maybe I still had a chance?*

"How are you?" he continued. "Have you wrapped many packages since we last saw each other?"

"Just a couple. I think I did a pretty good job, too. Thank you for the instruction."

"Well, I'm glad to hear it, and you're very welcome."

"My wife says I need to buy these couple of dress shirts, right, dear?" he said, turning to the woman who'd walked over to stand beside him. "But you'll be pleased to learn I don't need them wrapped."

*Wife? I guess I should have expected it.*

"Okay," I said as I turned, hopes deflated, to the register.

I rang up the purchase, handed him the bag and gave the customary farewell, "Thank you. Please come again."

"I will," he said as he locked arms with the petite blond and walked out of the store — and my dreams.

# Say Cheese

Cottage cheese on a bed of boring iceberg lettuce. Cottage cheese topped with sticky-sweet canned peaches. Cottage cheese with a crunchy side of Ry-Krisp. I could go on and on, but I'll bore you no further.

Suffice it to say, cottage cheese was consumed in abundance at our house. Mom often dieted; and, since my weight through adolescence fell a tad north of the normal range, she'd routinely recruit me to share in her latest determination to drop a few pesky pounds.

We both struggled with weight. My diminutive dad could be less than sympathetic. If we happened to be eating a normal amount at dinner time, he'd sometimes glare at one or the other of us with an expression that yelled, "You know you shouldn't be eating all that."

The crusade would begin again.

During one dedicated dieting marathon, I lost a paltry, unnoticeable five pounds while my mother dropped an astounding forty. She looked amazing. Her face shone with a glow of accomplishment.

The next Sunday morning, my father accompanied us to church — a rare occurrence. Mom looked beautiful in her brand new, fashionable, navy blue, drop waist dress with contrasting white cuffs and collar.

On the way up the steps into the sanctuary, a friend complimented her on her svelte appearance. Before Mom could respond, Dad turned to the woman and, with an expression of ultimate pride, said, "Yes, she does look wonderful, doesn't she?"

Mother's face lit with a broad smile as she blushed like a school girl. I got goose bumps. In that instant my heart filled with joy for my mother and overflowed with pride in my father.

I couldn't help but savor a moment worth more than all the cottage cheese in the world.

# Don't Let the Door . . .

"Can you believe it? We're about to graduate!"

"I know, but aren't you a little scared?" my bandmate asked. "It seemed like this day would never come and now high school is over. I have no clue what to do with the rest of my life."

"Well, I have to admit, I am a bit nervous. I planned to join the WACS. I thought it would be good experience and might help me decide what to do for a future career. My dad, however, refused to consider the idea. He said no daughter of his was going to enter the military. I guess having served during WWII himself and now with a son fighting in Vietnam, he figured that was enough service to our country."

"So what *are* you planning to do? College?"

"Not exactly. My folks can't afford it, and I didn't make enough money babysitting and working at the dime store to finance a college education. No, they have a different idea for my future."

"Oh? And what would that be?"

"Business college. I'm going to live with a family downtown and take a nine-month secretarial course. When I finish, I'll get a job through their placement office. Working as the family's maid will cover my room and board, and I'll be given bus fare to visit home every other weekend.

How about you? Is higher education in your future?"

"Nope, at least not right away. In a week or so, my boyfriend and I will be hitchhiking to California to be beach bums for a few months, or at least until he gets his draft notice. My folks are not thrilled, but I'm ready to make my own decisions."

"Wow, what a bold and exciting plan! I hope it works out for you."

"If it doesn't, it doesn't. Not the end of the world, I guess. At least I'm going to enjoy a good sendoff. My folks are throwing me a huge graduation party this weekend. How are you celebrating the momentous event?"

"Well, not with any big soirée, that's for sure. My parents don't believe in the whole party thing, never have. They're very pragmatic."

"You and your big words! Aren't you just saying they're cheap?"

"No. They simply feel it's a senseless expenditure for both host and attendees. They'll give me a gift tonight, though. It'll be something of necessity, I'm sure."

"I get it. But if you want to come hang out at my party, you're more than welcome."

"Thanks. I might. But we better stop talking now. The band is beginning Pomp and Circumstance; and, listen, they even sound okay without us in the trombone section."

Later in the evening, after celebratory cake and ice cream, Mom said, "It's time for your presents, Bonnie. Why don't you get comfortable on the couch and I'll bring them in."

A moment later, she slid a very large cardboard box in front of me and said, "But before you open this, we want to give you your other gift."

She handed me a small package encircled with shiny ribbon. Carefully, I loosened the tape and slid the contents from its wrapper. Opening the lid of the box, I stared at the sight of an elegant Elgin wristwatch with a gleaming, braided gold band and one tiny, sparkling gem in the center of the clock face.

"Oh, Mom, Dad, it's beautiful. Thank you so much. I'll wear it every day."

"You're very welcome, dear. Now open the big box, please."

"Okay. I can't wait to see what's in it!"

I grabbed the middle of the folded flaps and the box popped open to reveal the most practical of parting gifts — a three-piece set of hard-sided luggage.

"Thanks, Mom and Dad." I said with a polite yet perceptive smile.

My parents, with no words at all, sent a graduation message of utmost practicality: "Don't be late and ..." well, the suitcases communicated the conclusion.

I heard the window of my childhood slam shut and sensed a subtle shove through the door to adulthood.

# Epilogue

*Thank you for reading my words.*
*To all who survived spankings, jungle gyms,*
*car trips without seat belts, bicycle rides without helmets,*
*exposure to second-hand smoke,*
*drinking from the hose and playing with toy guns,*
*I raise my glass and say, "Salut! Job well done."*

*So as we brave baby-boomers stroll, shuffle,*
*limp or wheel through our remaining "golden" years*
*I encourage all to leave something tangible,*
*some written record of an amazing life lived*
*as a gift of utmost love and devotion*
*for future generations*
*to laugh at, learn from and cherish.*

"Every time you share your story, it's a
reminder that you've lived it and that it has value."

— Heather Greenwood Davis

# About the Author

Bonnie Papenfuss and her husband Larry moved from Maplewood, Minnesota to Green Valley, Arizona sixteen years ago to enjoy their retirement in the warmth and beauty of the Sonoran Desert. Though neither a teacher, both had life-long careers in the field of public education. Today Bonnie enjoys reading, writing, traveling, exploring nature and spending time with family and friends.

Her first book, *From the Window of God's Waiting Room: A Memoir of Playful Prose and Pleasant Poetry*, released in August of 2019, has been well-received with hundreds of copies sold throughout the United States and Canada.

Bonnie contributes a monthly book review for publication in the local newspaper and her poetry has been published in nine separate anthologies including the OASIS Journals of 2013 through 2017.

She is a long-time member of the Santa Cruz Valley Chapter of the Society of Southwestern Authors and a regular attendee of the Green Valley Writers Critique Forum.

Bonnie and her husband have a blended family of five grown daughters. They are the proud grandparents of six and great-grandparents of one.

You can contact her at lbpapenfuss1260@gmail.com.

Made in the USA
Middletown, DE
16 October 2020